CROSS-SECTIONS

THE EA–6B
PROWLER

by Ole Steen Hansen
illustrated by Alex Pang
Consultant: Craig Hoyle, Defense Editor, Flight International

Capstone
press
Mankato, Minnesota

First published in the United States in 2006 by Capstone Press
151 Good Counsel Drive, P.O. Box 669, Mankato, Minnesota 56002
http://www.capstonepress.com

Library of Congress Cataloging-in-Publication Data
Hansen, Ole Steen.
    The EA-6B Prowler / by Ole Steen Hansen ; illustrated by Alex Pang.
    p. cm.—(Edge books, cross-sections)
    Summary: "An in-depth look at the EA-6B Prowler, with detailed cross-section
diagrams, action photos, and fascinating facts"—Provided by publisher.
    Includes bibliographical references and index.
    ISBN 0-7368-5252-2 (hardcover)
    1. EA-6 (Electronic warfare aircraft)—Juvenile literature. 2. Airplanes,
Military—United States—Juvenile literature. I. Pang, Alex, ill. II. Title. III. Series.
UG1242.E43H37 2006
623.74'61—dc22   2005009640

Designed and produced by

David West ☂☂ Children's Books
7 Princeton Court
55 Felsham Road
Purney
London SW15 1AZ

Designer: Rob Shone
Editors: Gail Bushnell, Kate Newport

Photo Credits
U.S. Navy photo by Photographer's Mate 2nd Class Michael Watkins, 1, 10; Coral,6t,
7t; NASA, 6b; U.S. Navy photo by Mark J. Bebitas, 7b; U.S. Navy photo by Damon
J. Moritz, 11; U.S. Navy photo by Jayme Pastoric, 12-13t; U.S. Navy photo by Mark
Gleason, 12b; U.S. Navy photo by Bo Flannigan, 14, 28-29b; U.S. Navy photo by
Milosz Reterski, 15; U.S. Navy photo by Michael Sandberg, 16; U.S. Navy photo by
Lewis Hunsaker, 17; U.S. Navy photo by Paul J. Perkins, 18; U.S. Navy photo by
Ryan T. O'Connor, 21; Northrop Grummen, 22; U.S. Navy photo by Todd Frantom,
23; U.S. Navy photo by William Howell, 24; U.S. Navy photo by John E. Woods, 24-
25t; U.S. Navy photo by Joshua E. Helgeson, 26; DoD photo by David gossett, 18-
19t; Corbis, 29m.

1 2 3 4 5 6 10 09 08 07 06 05

TABLE OF CONTENTS

THE EA-6B PROWLER

The Prowler is a navy aircraft. It ensures that other aircraft are not located by enemy radar. Radar is equipment that uses radio waves to find or guide objects. Prowlers disrupt or jam enemy radar signals and destroy their radar. The enemy will then have a hard time defending itself against an attack.

Today, Prowler squadrons also support the U.S. Marines and the U.S. Air Force. Some EA-6B Prowlers fly from aircraft carriers, while others fly from land bases.

FIGHTING RADAR

Radar was first used during World War II (1939–1945). Radar has been used both to find aircraft and to prevent aircraft from being detected.

During World War II, bombers like this B-17 were vulnerable to attacks from fighters. Dropping chaff made it difficult for radar to help the fighters find the bombers.

CHAFF

Chaff are strips of metal foil released into the air to confuse a radar-controlled missile. It was one of the first methods used to disturb enemy radar signals during World War II.

DEFENSE SUPPRESSION

During the Vietnam War (1954–1975), some aircraft were given the job of destroying enemy radar and missile sites.

The F-105 Thunderchief was used as a Wild Weasel in Vietnam.

These aircraft were called Wild Weasels. Their radar-destroying missions were called defense suppression.

A-6 Intruders carried up to 22 bombs under their wings.

A-6 INTRUDER

The A-6 Intruder was one of the bombers used by the U.S. Navy in Vietnam. It was a strong aircraft capable of carrying heavy loads and flying in the worst weather. It was the forerunner of the Prowler in its overall design.

EA-6B PROWLER

In the 1960s, an improved version of the A-6 Intruder was developed. The EA-6B Prowler was designed to disrupt enemy radar signals. The Prowler entered service with the U.S. Navy in 1971.

A Prowler gets ready for an evening takeoff from an aircraft carrier.

CROSS-SECTION

The Prowler is a highly specialized aircraft. Its most important feature is its electronic jamming equipment.

Only 170 Prowlers have ever been built. The electronics are constantly updated so that these aircraft can continue to fly their missions. The Prowler has a crew of four and is designed to land on aircraft carriers.

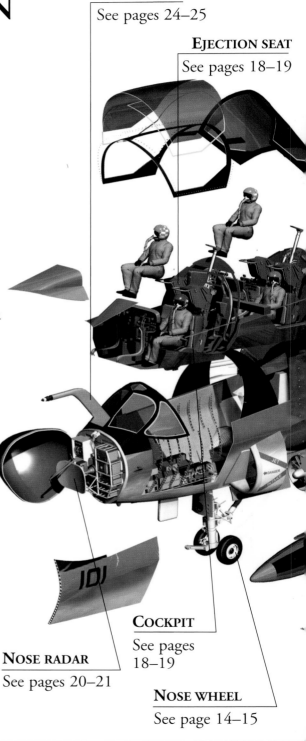

FUEL PROBE
See pages 24–25

EJECTION SEAT
See pages 18–19

NOSE RADAR
See pages 20–21

COCKPIT
See pages 18–19

NOSE WHEEL
See page 14–15

PROWLER FACTS
Wingspan: 53 feet (16.2 meters)
Length: 59 feet (18 meters)
Height: 15 feet (4.6 meters)
Speed: 651 miles (1,050 kilometers) per hour
Ceiling: 40,000 feet (12,200 meters)
Takeoff Weight: 61,500 pounds (27,900 kilograms)

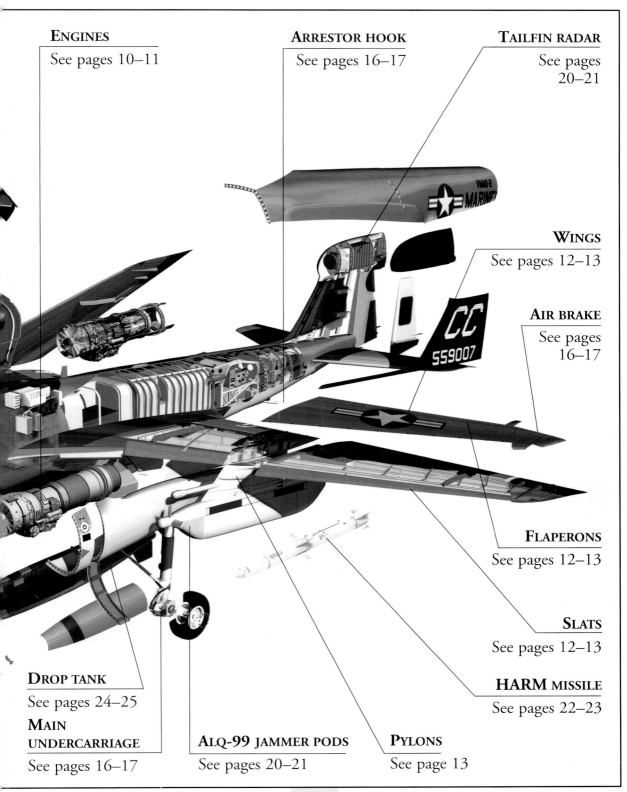

ENGINES
See pages 10–11

ARRESTOR HOOK
See pages 16–17

TAILFIN RADAR
See pages 20–21

WINGS
See pages 12–13

AIR BRAKE
See pages 16–17

FLAPERONS
See pages 12–13

SLATS
See pages 12–13

HARM MISSILE
See pages 22–23

DROP TANK
See pages 24–25

MAIN UNDERCARRIAGE
See pages 16–17

ALQ-99 JAMMER PODS
See pages 20–21

PYLONS
See page 13

VMAO-2 MARINES

CC
559007

THE ENGINES

The Prowler is powered by two jet engines. They are not as powerful as the engines on modern fighters.

The Prowler's engines are not designed to fly faster than the speed of sound. The Prowler cruises at the speed of a passenger jet. The exhausts of the engines are angled slightly downward. This helps the aircraft to take off from aircraft carrier decks.

Jet engines are reliable but require careful maintenance.

COMBUSTION CHAMBER
Fuel is burned in compressed air, which then expands rapidly.

INTAKE FAN
A fan at the front of the engine turns at high speed to suck in air.

COMPRESSOR
The compressor blades are mounted on the same shaft as the fan. They then compress the air.

Position of the engines on the Prowler

EXHAUST NOZZLE

The burning hot exhaust
leaves the aircraft, and the
aircraft is pushed forward.

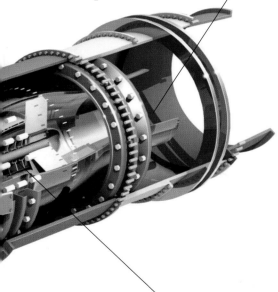

TURBINE

The expanding air forces its way
out toward the exhaust. The air
then hits the turbine blades and
turns them. The blades are
mounted on the same shaft as
the fan at the front, which then
sucks in more air.

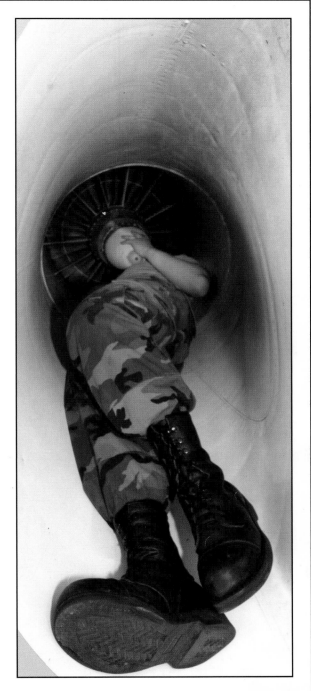

To check the fan blades, it is necessary
to crawl into the air intake duct. This
can only be done when the engine is
not running.

THE WINGS

The wings are needed to lift the Prowler. As the Prowler moves forward through the air, lift is created over its curved wings.

Air flowing past the wing must travel farther over the curved upper surface than under the flat lower surface. The upper air moves faster than the air below the wing. Faster-moving air creates lower air pressure. The higher air pressure under the wing holds the plane up with a force called lift.

The wings have flaps and slats. These parts can be lowered to create more lift during takeoff.

With the Prowler's folded wings, the wingspan is reduced to about 25 feet (8 meters).

Slats, flaps, and air brakes are deployed when the Prowler lands on its carrier.

LIFT
Air has to move faster over the curved top of the wing than on the underside. The higher speed of the air over the top of the wing creates lift. When the slats and flaps are lowered, more lift is created.

Flaperons and slats up

Lift

Air flow

Air flow

Flaperons and slats down

Greater lift

Air flow

Air flow

WING HINGES

FLAPERONS
A combination of flaps is needed for lift during takeoff and landing.

AIR BRAKES
The trailing edge of each wing splits open to become an air brake.

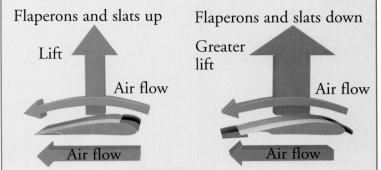

Position of folding wings on the Prowler

SLATS

PYLONS
Pylons under the wing are used to mount extra fuel tanks, missiles, or electronic equipment.

TAKEOFF

Taking off from an aircraft carrier is very difficult because the flight deck is so short. The Prowler must reach flying speed in only a few seconds.

The noise on the flight deck is so loud that hand signals must be used for all communications.

The Prowler uses a device called a shoe that is attached to the nose wheel.

SLATS

FLAPERONS

Flaps are lowered for takeoff to give more lift. Once in the air, the flaps are pulled up.

The Prowler engines are then run up to full power. A steam catapult shoots the shoe down the flight deck. The Prowler is then pulled along and hurled into the air.

Crew members are pressed back into their seats when the Prowler takes off.

NOSE WHEEL

The nose wheel must be strongly built because it has to whip the aircraft down the flight deck.

PAYLOAD

A typical payload for the Prowler includes three ALQ-99 jammer pods.

CATAPULT

The catapult is powered by steam. The blast deflector must be raised so the powerful takeoff doesn't damage other aircraft or injure the deck crew. The angled flight deck behind is used by landing aircraft.

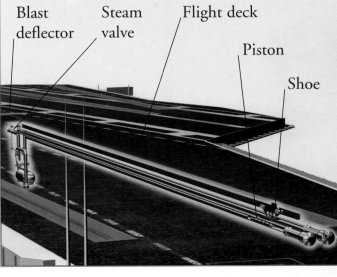

Blast deflector

Steam valve

Flight deck

Piston

Shoe

LANDING

Landing fast military jets on an aircraft carrier is not easy. In fact, it is one of the most challenging tasks a pilot has to face.

Carriers are huge ships, but their flight decks are much shorter than runways on land. The Prowler lowers an arrestor hook as it gets close to the carrier. This hook catches a wire on the flight deck. The wire and hook work together to slow down the aircraft.

In rough waters the flight deck moves up and down by 20 feet (6 meters) or more. Judging the landing is very difficult for the pilot.

ARRESTOR HOOK

AIR BRAKE

FLAPS

The Prowler slams onto the flight deck at a high speed. The main undercarriage must be strong enough to take the impact.

Here, the arrestor hook has just caught the wire. The pilot must apply full power at this point in case he doesn't catch the wire and has to go around and try once more. If the pilot is successful, the Prowler is stopped completely in a few seconds.

MAIN UNDERCARRIAGE

SLATS

622

NOSE WHEEL

THE COCKPIT

The Prowler has a crew of four. One pilot and three officers operate the electronic equipment.

The officer sitting next to the pilot operates the nose radar and the navigation systems. This officer also controls the systems that disturb enemy radio communications.

The two officers in the back seats operate the jamming systems. Their job is to make sure radar signals are disrupted and that the enemy has no warning and no chance to order a counter attack.

The Prowler stands tall on the flight deck. Pilots need stairs to get into the cockpit.

Position of cockpit on Prowler

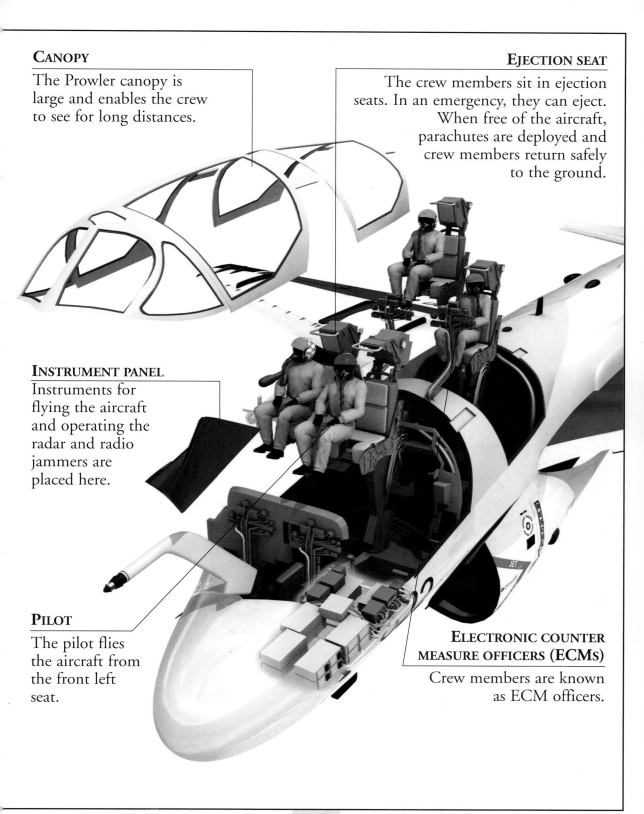

CANOPY

The Prowler canopy is large and enables the crew to see for long distances.

EJECTION SEAT

The crew members sit in ejection seats. In an emergency, they can eject. When free of the aircraft, parachutes are deployed and crew members return safely to the ground.

INSTRUMENT PANEL

Instruments for flying the aircraft and operating the radar and radio jammers are placed here.

PILOT

The pilot flies the aircraft from the front left seat.

ELECTRONIC COUNTER MEASURE OFFICERS (ECMs)

Crew members are known as ECM officers.

RADAR AND JAMMERS

The Prowler is equipped with powerful jammers that disturb enemy radar signals.

On top of the tailfin is a fairing that contains receivers. These receivers detect enemy radar signals. The Prowler crew members use the jammers to disrupt those signals. Radar may work with several different kinds of signals, so the jammers have to be able to disrupt all of them. This is why the Prowler has more than one jammer.

ELECTRONICS BAYS

The jamming system can be operated automatically by computers. The crew may also decide to work the jamming system manually.

RADAR

The radar in the Prowler nose is used for navigation. Prowler crew members need to know exactly where they are at all times so they can support friendly aircraft.

ALQ-99 JAMMER POD

The Prowler usually flies with a jammer pod under each wing and one under the fuselage. This Prowler is also equipped with a fuel drop tank under each wing.

Position of radar and jammers on the Prowler

TAILFIN RECEIVERS

The tailfin fairing is called "the football." It houses the receivers that locate the signals from the enemy radar.

JAMMING

The main purpose of the Prowler is to jam enemy radar. The enemy is "blind" to attack.

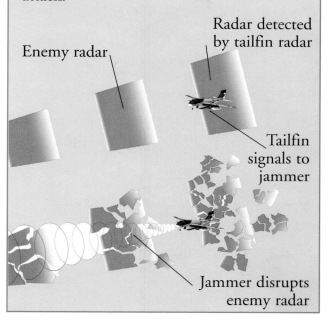

Enemy radar

Radar detected by tailfin radar

Tailfin signals to jammer

Jammer disrupts enemy radar

The jammers need electric power. During flight, the small propeller at the front is turned by the wind. This propels a generator that produces electricity.

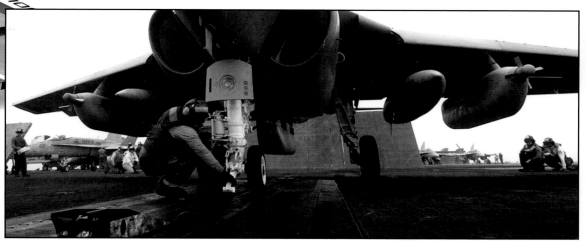

HARM MISSILE

At first, the Prowler was only a jammer aircraft. But in the 1980s, Prowlers were armed with HARM missiles.

HARM missiles zero in on enemy radar signals. They automatically find the radar site and destroy it. When a Prowler flies near a radar site, the enemy has to choose between switching off the radar or having it destroyed.

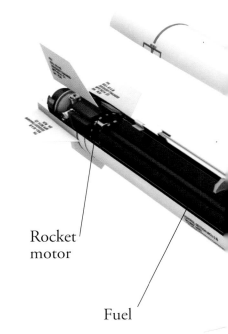

Rocket motor

Fuel

Armed with two HARM missiles, the Prowler has become an effective weapon against enemy radar sites.

HARM MISSILE

New versions of the HARM missiles "remember" where the enemy radar is, even if it is switched off. The HARM will still find and destroy it.

Staff working with weapons such as the HARM missile wear red jackets on the flight deck so that they can be seen clearly.

Warhead

Fins

Autopilot electronics

Guidance electronics

Radome

Even if the Prowler does not destroy the radar, it has provided the necessary support to other attacking aircraft. The enemy cannot detect them because the radar is not working.

Position of HARM missile on Prowler

AIR-TO-AIR REFUELING

Sometimes tanker aircraft refuel a Prowler in the air. Air-to-air refueling requires careful formation flying.

Air-to-air refueling is necessary when a Prowler has to fly long distances. Prowlers might fly from a base in the United States to the Middle East. The S-3B Viking is a tanker aircraft that is used to refuel planes such as the Prowler. Air-to-air refueling is particularly difficult if it takes place at night or in bad weather.

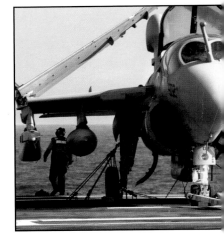

This Prowler has fuel drop tanks on the inboard pylons under the wing.

A Prowler is refueled in the air by a S-3B Viking.

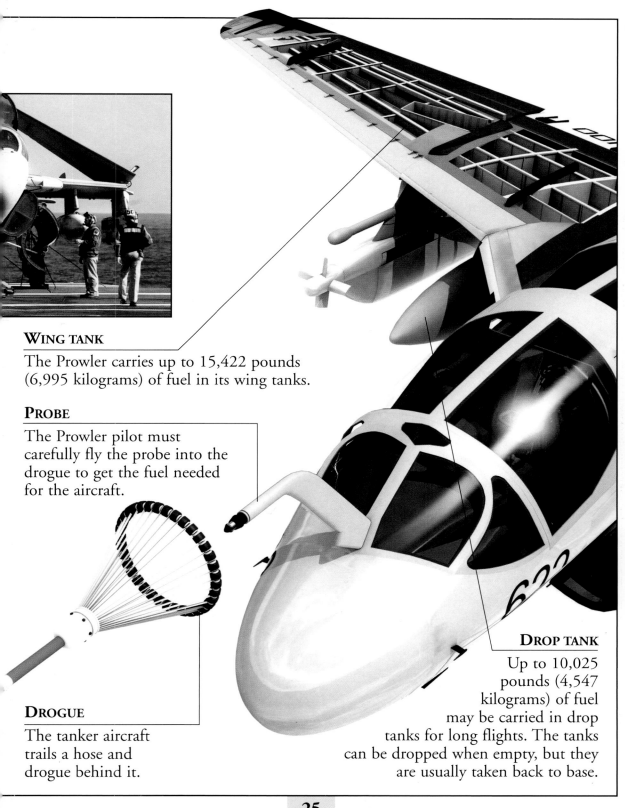

WING TANK

The Prowler carries up to 15,422 pounds (6,995 kilograms) of fuel in its wing tanks.

PROBE

The Prowler pilot must carefully fly the probe into the drogue to get the fuel needed for the aircraft.

DROGUE

The tanker aircraft trails a hose and drogue behind it.

DROP TANK

Up to 10,025 pounds (4,547 kilograms) of fuel may be carried in drop tanks for long flights. The tanks can be dropped when empty, but they are usually taken back to base.

THE MISSION

The Prowler's mission is to support other aircraft by jamming enemy radar.

A Prowler is sent out to support an attack by F/A-18s. A Hawkeye radar aircraft is also part of the mission. The Prowler crew members rarely see the aircraft they support.

1. The Prowler takes off from its aircraft carrier.

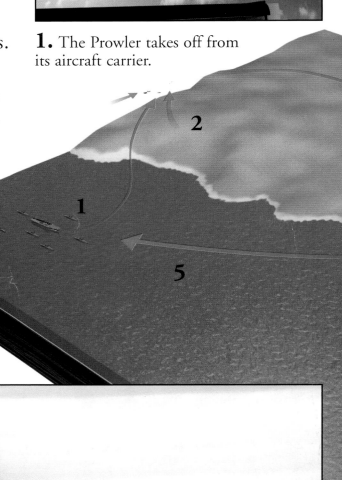

Two support aircraft of the U.S. Navy, the Prowler and the Hawkeye. The radar on top of the Hawkeye can track hundreds of ships and aircraft at the same time.

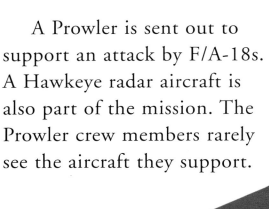

2. The Hawkeye radar aircraft is also in the air to watch out for enemy aircraft. The F/A-18s are briefly seen on their way to bomb enemy tanks.

3. The Prowler detects and jams the enemy radar transmission. The enemy is prevented from detecting the F/A-18s.

3

4

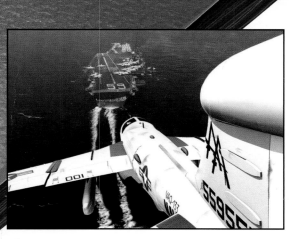

5. The Prowler returns to the carrier.

4. One enemy radar site is destroyed using HARM missiles.

THE FUTURE

The Prowler is the only aircraft used just for the jamming and suppression of enemy defense aircraft in the U.S. military today. It will stay in service for many years to come.

Other U.S. aircraft, like the F-16, attack radar sites with HARM missiles, but only the Prowler can also detect and jam their signals. The Prowler is an old aircraft. Faster and more modern aircraft may someday take over.

The roar of Prowler engines can be heard on U.S. flight decks around the world.

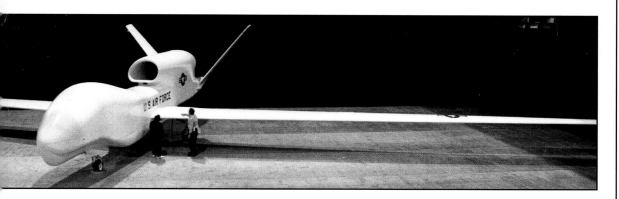

In the future some defense suppression
missions will be flown by unmanned aircraft.

The Prowler will eventually be replaced by a
variant of the F-18 (*above*). The new EA-18G
will be able to do all the things that the
Prowler can do.

Some new aircraft will be flown
unmanned. They can then be used to
fly some missions without risking the
lives of any crew.

GLOSSARY

aircraft carrier (AIR-kraft KA-ree-ur)—a warship with a flight deck where aircraft take off and land

canopy (KAN-uh-pee)—the cover over an airplane cockpit

chaff (CHAF)—strips of metal foil released into the air to confuse a radar-controlled missile

exhaust (eg-ZAWST)—heated air leaving a jet engine

fairing (FAIR-ing)—an external compartment on an aircraft that can hold various features while keeping the outline smooth and streamlined

fuselage (FYOO-suh-lahzh)—main part of a plane where the crew or passengers sit

mission (MIH-shuhn)—a task given to a person or group

radar (RAY-dar)—equipment that uses radio waves to find or guide objects

squadron (SKWAHD-ruhn)—a group of aircraft that go on a mission together

thrust (THRUHST)—the force that pushes an aircraft forward

READ MORE

Hansen, Ole Steen. *Air Combat.* The Story of Flight. New York: Crabtree, 2004.

Shuter, Jane. *War Machines: Military Vehicles Past and Present.* Travel Through Time. Chicago: Raintree, 2004.

Sweetman, Bill. *Radar Jammers: The EA-6B Prowlers.* War Planes. Mankato, Minn.: Capstone Press, 2002.

INTERNET SITES

FactHound offers a safe, fun way to find Internet sites related to this book. All of the sites on FactHound have been researched by our staff.

Here's how:
1. Visit *www.facthound.com*
2. Type in this special code
   0736852522
   for age-appropriate sites. Or enter a search word related to this book for a more general search.
3. Click on the **Fetch It** button.

FactHound will fetch the best sites for you!

INDEX